BRIGHT MORNING

Jane Seabourne

BRIGHT MORNING

✦

OFFA'S PRESS

2012

First published 2010 by Offa's Press,
Ferndale, Pant, Oswestry, Shropshire, SY10 9QD
Reprinted 2012

ISBN: 978–0–9565518–0–1

Typeset in Baskerville Old Face

Designed by Début, Wolverhampton

Printed and bound by Steatham's,
Wombourne, Staffordshire

Contents

Carpe Noctem   7
At the Family Fun Day   8
Perfume   9
Evanescence   11
Orange Wednesday   12
The Way Home   13
The Seventh Wife   14
Oblations   15
What I Know   16
In Morecambe   17
Black Magic   18
Feathers   19
At the Discovery Centre   20
Demeter Dreams of Jam   21
Echoes   22
Big Garden Birdwatch   23
For One Night Only   24
Portraits with the Family Comb   25
Potted Anger   26
Sometimes, in these her days of Pleasant Confusion   27
A Brief History of Garlic   28
Love Song   29
Double Zoo.   31
Six Things they said about Cholera   32
Buttons   33
When he was Ten   34
After the Operation   36
Bright Morning   37
Tadeusz and the Mice   38
Those Gloves   40
Odd Frogs and Old Gloves   41

Mappa Mundi   42

The 9.05 to Paddington, is, as ever, full   44

Red Kites   45

Staircases   46

The Great Dustbinian Formation   47

What Love is Like   48

Ornithopter   49

On Going to Lunch with Friends:
One of the Guests Brings Polly, Aged Five Weeks   50

Falling   51

Earth   52

Fishing   53

Nos Galan   54

The Fire-Eater's House   55

I Try Your House on Like Old Clothes   56

Dr Johnson   57

St Cuthbert   58

Strawberry Thief   59

Hand Grenades   60

How to Remember   61

Carpe Noctem

Sashaying arm-in-arm through clubs and bars
They razzle-dazzle in their spike-heeled shoes,
Spaghetti-strappy tops and push-up bras,
Low-slung hipsters show G-strings and tattoos
And pierced navels. Drop-dead gorgeous groups
Ricochet round dance-floor, bar and loos,
Propelled by power that never flags nor droops
(or vodka shots and multi-coloured booze).
Armed to the teeth with lip gloss, cash and comb
They party 'til the last bar closes down,
Wolfing hot-dogs as they swagger home –
On Fridays, when the girls go on the town.
Rip-roaring girls, you're diamond hard and bright:
You reach out with both hands and seize the night.

At the Family Fun Day

Clowns with size 20 shoes patter over the
remnants of the lawn cadging lights from
androgynous types in furry parrot suits
before the furry parrots square up to
Sumo wrestlers in *It's a Knock Out*
scheduled for twelve noon after the
celeb. hairdresser makeover in the hall and
before the cook-off in the car park.

It's rumoured there will be morris dancing
but that was put about by the Engineers
who don't want to be there anyway.
Senior staff look sheepish in tee shirts and
fixed smiles. They give out goody bags and
helium filled balloons with logos to children
painted as butterflies or tiger-cubs and
who are considering a tantrum.

Even the man in the green jumper, believed to be
the principal, is powerless to prevent a play the
Performing Arts students wrote themselves -
a contemporary take on a Greek tragedy.
Tiger-cubs and butterflies are pushed over the edge.
The DJ interrupts his request programme
on the radio station rigged up in the front lobby
asking the First Aiders to make themselves known.

Those with unusual perseverance manage,
by the end of the family fun day,
to enrol on a course for the autumn term.

Perfume

Through smoke
prayers rise.
From altar candles,
incense burners,
votive stands.
Funnelled through
church spires,
spiralled round
onion domes,
coiled from shrines and
temples
prayers are sent
upwards.
Through frankincense,
and rosemary,
and sandalwood:

Bless my crops
Let them believe
Make me well
Give us a son
Fetch him home
Stop this war
Bring me luck
Save our souls
Marry me.

Prayers rise
through smoke.

Through smoke -
Per fumare.

Through perfume
prayers rise.
On earlobes, wrists,
crooks of knees,
from cut glass bottles,
atomised through air,

smeared from
stoppered flasks
prayers are sent
outwards.
Through Givenchy,
through Cinnabar,
through Shalimar:
Return my calls:
Visit soon
Leave your wife
Think of me
Stay with me
Make me smile
Restore my looks
Keep me young
Marry me.

Through perfume and
through smoke
prayers rise.

And the sending is
more valid than the
answering for those
who purge their
helplessness in
the rising of prayer
through perfume and
through smoke.

Evanescence

The dog turd at the bus stop
took a little while to decompose.

It was, at first, the smell that
caused comment. An odd concoction
of cream and meat,
hitting the back of the throat and
hard to get out of the nose.

A sharp frost saw that off.
Rain, bacterial activity
and, of course, time did the rest.

There was shrinkage
followed by mummification
and eventually, it was gone.

Even then, there was a darker patch,
a silhouette, like an outline drawn
around a corpse at a murder scene.

That lingered for weeks.
When, by late spring,
that too disappeared, I fancied the
weeds grew there more vigorously
than before.

Of you, my darling, there is no trace,
no lingering scent, substance,
damp patch, shape,
no souvenir, no lasting benefit.
Nothing even, to write home about,
or turn into small talk
at a bus stop.

Orange Wednesday

He's like a junk-shop sofa now,
horse-hair sprouts out of his ears and nose.

Lighting up his morning cigarette,
prehensile bristles detect a whiff

of orange-peel and sweet tobacco smoke,
and it's a black-out tram-ride back –

the Picture Palace and a Friday night.
Humphrey Bogart with his bottle blondes,

and in the one-and-nines, a hand goes north,
passing the border of a stocking-top,

one last rasp of his apprentice hands
and he crosses into Hollywood,

the glamour of bare skin. He splashes out –
a carton of Kiaora squash, a Woodbine

offered nonchalantly in the blue-haze dark.
Bogie looks at him from the screen and winks.

The Way Home

…is not straightforward
as the crow might boast.
From Aston Eyre past
Morville Hall the
road cavorts.
In Corve Vale,
a blowsy barmaid
beguiles us with her
country wiles. Nothing
is as it seems.
At Wormbridge
there be dragons.
Kilpeck's corbels
spread their legs and
cock a snook at
prissy Christians.
A Norman castle
keeps back rebel
Welsh and puts the English
in their place.
But the border is not so easily
put down, more a thumb-rule than
a plumb-bobbed line.
Border people lead such double lives.
The devil launched
himself off Skirrid and
a saint was made on a
hangman's rope in
Usk - my journey's end.
Too much time and
many tides have turned
to find the way back easy.
Still, the air is clean as gin
upon the tongue,
which is, they say,
the speech of heaven,
and sound enough
to call the wayward home…

The Seventh Wife

He said: *use any key but this.*

She murmured underneath her breath;
He let her think she was unwatched.
She slipped the key between her breasts;
It stamped its shape upon her skin.
She stroked it with a bride's caress;
She held it to her florid mouth.
It left a mark as cold as death;
She shivered with delicious fear.
She smoothed her rustling silken dress –
She crossed her fingers twice for luck –
She tip-tapped on the passage floor –
She slid the key into the lock.

He felt the roar of blood once more.

Oblations

October, and I am drawn to
the rose-red rosary of yew berries
unthreading daily from my tree.

As I was by the pocket-money box of beads
that cost a silver sixpence.

In shape, all perfect oblates.

I wanted to eat them.

I did not know how else
to express my devotion.

What I Know

To know: a verb with a vigorous life The Oxford English Dictionary

I know a lot, according to my CV,
which lists examinations I have passed,
including maths, it seems.

I know, thanks to my mother,
how to make pastry short and sponge-cakes rise.

I know (but have no proof), that God is dead,
that when I die, I'll walk a corridor
with matt emulsion walls, and when I reach the end,
I'll find a door and open it onto oblivion.

On the other hand, I know, without a doubt
my parents are in heaven, where my mother
puts her poor feet up at last,
and my father has eternal membership
of the celestial rugby club.

I know, or have known, biblically,
the ins and outs of several men. Except
my former husband, who was, in so many ways
unknowable.

I know I am prone to exaggerate.

I know April is not the cruellest month –
September is. Ask any teacher.

I know I have good points,
but where compliments are concerned, to give is better,
and to receive is to handle stolen goods.

I know I that for every sore, I have a plaster,
which is good, because, being so sharp,
the danger is I'll cut myself.
I know I once was 'clear winter'
but now have faded to a subtler time of year.
I know I never have been cool, preferring
The Beatles to The Stones; tea to coffee;
white wine to red; early mornings to late nights
and poetry that tends toward the beautiful.

In Morecambe

The sea parades in shot-silk evening gowns –
blue or pewter, depending on her mood –
flounced out with petticoats of spume and lace,
hemline stiff with sand, dragging on the ground;

wears necklaces of sailors' knucklebones
(pearls, she thinks, are common and too dull);
her stockings, finest fifteen-denier kelp,
so flimsy, they gather round her knees in rolls.

In spring, she fixes fishing nets into a shawl
and twirls them in her wine-dark hair.
On winter nights, she steals a reefer coat
and weights the pockets with pebbles and fine shale.

Her eyes have lighthouse lenses: off and on.
They seem to say: *the sea is in her, stay away.*

Black Magic

At eighteen Park Street, life was black and white
as bible print on tablecloths. Stale bread
with lumps of coal was all we had to eat,
and fibbing little girls were seen not heard.

One day, a stranger came and handed round
a box of sweets. To be polite, I took
a strawberry cream, but let it bloom with mould
(I pressed the foil inside a story-book).

The wrapping clearly meant for looking through
transformed our garden mud with pink and rose.
The ice floes in the puddles melted to
a crimson lake. I shed my winter clothes.

In Park Street's monochrome, I grew aware
of wonder, and, as lights went on, despair.

Feathers

When they lived at home, they slept top to toe –
Marion, Olwen, Bronwen, Joy –
in the iron bedstead, on the sprouting
mattress, blue-striped bolsters head and foot,
china pot below, above, a text in poker work:
The Lord Is Watching Over You.

The four girls laughed there till they cried.
Their father – Baptist convert that he was –
would bellow up the Alpine stairs: *What are*
you doing up there? Which set them off again.
It's only feathers, dad, stuck in our throats,
they whispered, mouths fluttering,
eyes half-closed and brimming, hardly fit
to speak for giggles.

Please say her God is watching still,
over this Home, where our youngest aunt
sits dozing in her Velcroed slippers,
hair a dandelion clock, and let her real self be
in that place where time went AWOL
somewhere in the 'twenties,
and she is still upstairs at home,
laughing with the girls at feathers gone adrift.

At the Discovery Centre

In their display case,
leaf-cutter ants
lunch on pink geraniums.

A woman plays
'Catch a Falling Star'
on a giant piano, with her feet.

Under the infra-red camera,
my armpits glow orange,
the rest of me is green.

A plastic model shows
how vowel sounds are produced:
Aargh, I mouth to myself.

On a half-sized torso,
you reassemble body parts,
inserting the heart back to front.

I discover I am leaving you.

Demeter Dreams of Jam

Demeter feels the nights draw in
and dreams of jam. It's hardly light
she's out there in the garden picking fruit,
pulling at the brambles,
scram-marks up her weathered arms,
tearing branches, berries, leaves, and all,
till every piece of Tupperware she owns is full.

Demeter turns the kitchen into hell.
Before Jim Naughtie says *Welcome to 'Today'*,
she's reached the setting point.
She lines up rows of Kilner jars; ladles in
her glut; scribbles labels; slaps on lids –
no time for them to cool.

Demeter hardly registers the lethal heat,
holding up a jar, convincing herself
she's trapped in what she can of summer:
sunlight; sweetness; leaves and thorns;
a wasp or two, wonderful and venomous –
the essence of the Upper Ground.

Demeter fits as many bottles as will go into a box,
stands it next the cases in the hall,
and waits until her daughter wakes
to pack the luggage in the car, and take her back
to what they now must think of as her other home.

Echoes

In this old house
I've heard them.
Echoing in the chimney,
railing at the floorboards,
whispering through the mortar.

There's sobbing
from the rafters,
whimpering
from the scullery,
screaming
from the space between
the wainscot and the wall.

From the coilings
of my ears,
the cavern
of my ribcage,
from the liver and lights of me,
I fetch up the
voices of children
buried in this old house.

Big Garden Birdwatch

27—28 January 2007

I saw:

- A couple of house sparrows
- 3 blackbirds inc. one female
- A blue tit swinging from the washing line
- 2 magpies. True, I only found the second by scanning trees with my binoculars.

Which was how I saw the seagull,
watching us, clocking:

- 11 cyclists in yellow lycra, blue helmets, looking like a flock of mobile great tits
- A gaggle of Wolves supporters (in winter plumage)
- 5 common humans flocking round a car for sale, cooing.
- 1 feral man, behind a garden shed, having a crafty smoke.

For One Night Only

"Enjoy the view, I did."
One of many inscriptions on benches at South Bay, Scarborough.

The ones who loved this place, the Addersons,
the Marshalls, and Fred Parks, are only waiting for

the drumroll of the overture to leave
their graves, take up the benches kept for them

in South Bay's glamorous dress circle. It's show-time
and the Harzigs, Metcalfs, Dennis Foy of York,

applaud themselves for shrewd investing
in the calibre of family and close friends

who reserved them the best seats in the house
for the end-of-pier turn to beat them all.

The chaps wear overcoats and natty trilbies,
their lady wives knot headscarves under chins

and ease the tops off Thermos flasks to pour
out tea with 'summat strong enough', to beat the chill.

They wouldn't want to catch their deaths out there,
the Caygills, Fosters and Bobbie Lodge,

who used to walk these paths with his dog, Star.
They're waiting, this most select of houses,

passing round a box of Orchard Fruits,
ready for the Lord to come and top the bill.

Portraits with the Family Comb

No oil paintings, but here we are – the Seabournes –
depicted in the glass above the kitchen range,
having our private moments with the comb.

Our father, anointing an ebbing tide of waves
with brilliantine. Burning corks to turn
the clock back on his yellowing moustache.

Our mother, raking through a greying perm
with wash-day hands. No dawdling: she knows
look too long and the devil will look back.

My brother, fingering his art-school beard,
eye closed, thumb out, planning his masterpiece:
'Portrait of the Artist Looking Cool '.

And me, slightly foxed by mousy hanks
of rat's tail hair, trying out a Beatle cap
for style. Look, if you can't be blonde, beguile…

Potted Anger

(an old-fashioned dish, best eaten cold)

She waited for low-tide
to walk out on the sands and pick
a crateful of reticulated shells.

She boiled them till they turned
sclerotic pink
and simmered them.

She spiced them with cayenne,
a scrape of nutmeg, mace,
shook in some chilli flakes.

She dipped her finger in –
to taste. It needed something more:
a grating of her favourite flavour,

which was malice. When cool,
she potted up the mix,
spooned over molten butter –

to keep it fresh. One day,
he roared out to be fed.
And then she let him have it,
spread on good and thick.

Sometimes, in these her days of Pleasant Confusion

She remembers where she left her teeth,
recites the genealogy of neighbours back to Adam,
recalls with lyrical clarity the day
she saw an aeroplane for the first time.

Some days she tells anyone who'll listen
she's never been undressed by a man.

Some days she wears two bras.

Some days she'll tell you straight off
the day of the week and
the name of the prime minister.

Some days, she picks up the thread of a story
about a woman she knew with withered ovaries
but it peters out before the end.

And some days, she only gives away
her mother's maiden name and Co-op number.

A Brief History of Garlic

They say that garlic first grew in hollows
Satan made with his left foot as he strolled,
Whistling, out of Eden.

The well-manured imprints were perfect
Bedding for the wayward scapes and purple
Mop-top heads, so full of *joie-de-vivre,*
They practically invite a passer-by
To go down on both knees and delve into
The loam with their bare hands, uproot the bulbs
And take them to their hearts.

Then, anyone would want to know what happens
If you leave them in darkness till they dry
And when you bring them out, they are so white,
So tempting, you cannot help yourself. You'd
Simply have to undo their outer skin,
Close in colour to kid-gloves, and tender–
Like a lady's underthings.

And once inside, your poor heart aches to see
The variegated cloves all snuggled up,
Damp as new-born babes, begging to be cleaved
Apart, and you choose one fat lobe to hold –
From utter curiosity.

And when you crush it, even though the stench
Released reeks more like corpses than roses,
Because you are Eve's offspring, you have to
Eat it to find out if it is like Hell –
All wind and sulphur – or the condiment
You pine for to restore the piquancy
You have not tasted in any mouthful
Since the day before the fall.

Love Song

(for a man with a hundred pairs of glasses)

Because I love you, I will help you find
your favourite glasses, even though when I
bought varifocals, you looked at them and said: *How much!*
and said you could buy a hundred pairs for that
in T J Hughes, or T K Maxx. And did.

So, now you have a hundred two-pound pairs,
and amongst them are your favourites, which are lost,
and even though I want to strangle you,
because I love you, I will help you find
your favourite glasses. The hunt begins.

First, we eliminate the obvious:
the silver metal ones propped in your hair,
the ones hung on a lanyard round your neck,
those lined up in your pocket with your pens
for they are not your favourites. We progress:

we find your second bests beside the bed,
the one-armed ones you use for stirring tea,
the ones like Ronnie Corbett wore turn up
with the remote. One lost thing found at least.

We find your shaving glasses by the phone,
your drinking glasses in the cellar, with the wine,
your outside loo ones dangling on a chain,
the pair repaired with tape is in the shed,
you like them, but they are not your favourites.

And so we look some more and find the half-moon pair
you wear to look intelligent, and those
with thin green arms like lizards' legs,
the leopard prints, I say are ladies' frames,
you say are camouflage. In backs of drawers
some day-glo ones stare back, and make us jump.

I plunge my arm between the sofa seats,
retrieve your lucky lottery specs, a pack
of furry peppermints and forty p.

In the spare room, a red pair has mated
with a yellow pair: they have orange offspring,
which is getting warmer, but not hot.

Your favourite glasses are tango plastic
trimmed in black, they have a raffish air
and are the self-same ones the size four blondie
in the coffee shop says give you the look
of some heart-throb off the tele that she thinks is fit.
You forget his name, but know for certain
he can't be more than thirty-five at most.

Which makes your day, makes them your favourites,
which you've lost somewhere in this house…

and because I love you, I will help you find
your favourite glasses.

Double Zoo.

Loreto Oxbridge girls have double zoo.,
their chaperones are Sister Gertrude and forty jars
of bloodless specimens preserved in alcohol.

Quick hands make heavy work of spatchcocked frogs.
The air is three parts chloroform, one dust.
Indifferent insects couple in their tanks.

Time's an elastic thread that snaps at last,
releasing girls from class (and navy drawers).
They hitch their skirts mid-thigh, cadge cigarettes,

en route to the Kardomah coffee bar
to raise the heart-rate of Xavarian boys,
and see first-hand the surge and flush of blood.

Six Things they said about Cholera

*i.m. Elizabeth Dawson of Temple Street, Bilston, who took ill at 10.00 pm on
August 3rd, 1832, having eaten a supper of pig's fry, and died at 5.00 am
on August 4th, the first of 682 deaths from cholera in the following six weeks.*

Firstly, it was a predicament.
A pestilence ravaging France, Spain,
Hungary, Prussia, lately docked in Sunderland,
arriving in Bilston like a thief i'the night.

Secondly, it was a visitation, spread by
Godlessness and uncleanly habits,
profligacy and drunkenness, and,
as observed in Temple Street,
sleeping fifteen to a room.

Thirdly, the symptoms were diverse:
giddiness; cramp at toe- and finger-tips;
vomiting; leaden-blue skin; rapid pulse;
sunken eyes with an expression
one could only describe as electro-plated.

Moreover, the prognosis was lamentable:
three to twelve hours.
Few survive.

Remedies, however, were legion
roast-beef; stale bread; brandy; laudanum;
ammonia; boiling water; hot bricks;
grains of disinfectant powder; and at 6d the packet,
Daffy's Genuine Elixir.

The solutions therefore, were obvious:
immediate burial at six-feet or more
and denouncements from the pulpit against
profligacy and drunkenness
and sleeping fifteen to a room.

Buttons

The character alone, stage right
at the curtain call
is the one I cheer the loudest,

the archetype
of oddbods and goosegogs,

frogged and shanked,
salt-marked with tears,
faithful as old Towser,

knows his place, below stairs,
with the chamoix and ash cans,

growing show-stopping pumpkins,
fattening a cellarful of mice,

eating cheese to dream up scenes
where she's in need
and he kneels down before the fire,
warming those old slippers,
rubbing her heels where her new shoes pinch.

When he was Ten

The boy was ten when strange things first appeared
behind the loose bricks in the garden wall –

his secret hiding-place for treasure trove,
so secret only he knew it was there.

His first find was a shrivelled mass of stuff,
the mummified remains of something odd.

Beside it was a note in purple ink,
addressed to him, and asking: *What is this?*

It took a week before he found someone
to tell him how gall-wasps make oak-apples –

he left his answer in the hiding place,
and soon it was replaced with other things:

once, the skull and neck bone of a finch:
so frail, he hardly dared to pick it up.

Among his other finds: an almond shell,
with teeth marks where a rat had gnawed inside;

a rotting elder branch with fungus growths
like disembodied jellied human ears.

In autumn, a clutch of chestnuts curled,
like day-old baby hedgehogs, only green.

He pulled apart the pellet of an owl
to find mouse bones and undigested fur.

Sometimes he found true beauties – broad bean pods
enclosed pink seeds with speckles of jet black.

The boy thought if he ever had a wife,
she'd wear a necklace made of beads like that.

Another time a piece of sculpted card
turned out to be a section of wasps' nest.

He found from broken shells that blackbirds' eggs
are speckled brown, and robins' eggs are blue,

that sparrow-hawks can sever wings of larks
by snapping cleanly through their feather shafts,

that tadpoles change to frogs in sixteen weeks,
but lichen can take years to grow an inch.

He learned about the cycle of the year
and that all living things will one day die,

The day he turned eleven, his last find,
a magnifying glass and empty book.

On the fly-leaf in purple oak-gall ink:
Here is the note book of a naturalist.

After the Operation

Our mother's other breast
was moon-glow white.
It had a pleasant heft.

She kept it in a box
with all the unused things
she said she kept for best.

Bright Morning

It wasn't Marmite or The Archers
Eurydice missed most,
of all things, it was pink.

Not your day-glos, lipsticks, bubble-gums,
the hot and shocking pinks
she favoured in her youth –

more tongue-tip, cheek-blush, ear-lobe,
inner-wrist. But most of all she missed
the pink of sunrise and bright morning.

Tadeusz and the Mice

The mice are back. His neck-hair bristles as
they do the polka over table-tops
and leave their evil foot prints pressed into
the butter he forgot to put away,
deposit *guwna* on the quarry tiles.
The *peppered* mice are back. He feels alive.

Time was, he'd swat them with a broom, or catch
a cat to fight them, Coliseum-wise.
His cat entrapping days are well past now,
but crafty still, he sets off for his shed.
Among the boxes of carbolic soap;
a winter's worth of cabbage; balls of twine;
the gears and wheels of broken bicycles;
behind encrusted tools, he finds the heap
of snares called *little paws* – this takes all day.

That night, the man whose life has been defined
by enemies – the Nazis, army rules,
the Russians; no-good *Łempki* from Ukraine –
lays mouse-traps all along the kitchen floor.
The man who witnessed Stalin's son quick-marched
through Krakow, understands revenge, concocts
a vision of himself, his fist outstretched,
displaying lifeless *myszy* by their tails.
Though, if he were a more reflective type,
the man who does things in his own sweet way,
might think that other people had a point
and baiting traps with food would do the trick.

Then, had he been the kind to think things through,
he would have come to England, like his wife,
with solid gold to pay their way. Instead,
he hid thick wads of saved up dollar bills
below the floor-boards in the hall. A space
the mice already called their own. They thanked
their benefactor for his handsome gift
of such fine lining stuff with broods and broods

of mouselings. So many generations
he swears that they will witness his last rites,
this worst and best of enemies, the mice.

Tadeusz – pronounced 'Tad-ay-oosh'
guwna – 'guvna', shit
peppered – English translation of a Polish oath
little paws—literal translation of the Polish for mouse trap
Łempki –'*Wempki*'. The 'no-goods'.
myszy –'*mishy*', mice

Those Gloves

The jiffy bag arrived
with nothing
but a pair of opera gloves
and the handwritten imperative:
enjoy!

On winter nights,
before the dressing-table mirror
sitting in my fur-trimmed mules,
I roll down those recycled gloves,
re-roll the turned back edge,
ease the leather up my arms,
stroking the second skin they are,
remarking to no-one in particular that
as there is no smoke in public now,
without a secret smoulderer
craving somewhere in the room,
so, how hidden from us are our true desires.

Odd Frogs and Old Gloves

The worldly goods I love
are all, in some way, odd:
the mottled, piebald, skewed,
things lop-sided and left behind.

Take this terracotta frog –
a garden ornament –moulded
in two halves. Sold discounted,
a pound or two at most.

Bought, forgotten, lost,
found today, burrowed
in soil double-dug
for this year's bean-trench.

Looks like winter soaked
the porous surface, froze.
When the spring thaw came
half its face broke away, one flank.

Sometime, a colony of lichen
took hold of this buried treasure:
covered a rounded back,
the remaining haunch,

brought about a sort of verdigris.
The same high-art finish
I've seen on statues in public squares,
thought valuable there.

My hand –warm as an old glove –
cups this frog, pockets it.
Now it is particular,
I count it good enough to love.

Mappa Mundi

To find out how we got from there to here,
I drew, with careful mapping pen, the world
as it appeared in nineteen-fifty-eight.

Jerusalem is eighteen Park Street – two-up,
two-down, no view, the centre of the Earth,
all compass points are sun-rays from the step,
and east is to the right as you look out.

The furthest east is number twenty-two,
where Aunty Mary Miles and Uncle Ivor
lived with Claerwen, their grown-up son,
who gave his old bike to my older brother, Pete.

Westward, Aunty Palser lived with gas-light,
a stuffed ram's head above the pantry door,
and wood-worm in her front-room furniture.

My brother's friends, Aubrey, Noel,
the Spencers –John and Jeff –
Gethin Mapstone with his imaginary horse,
patrolled the frontier.

The corner house was bigger than the rest,
with room enough for Mr Hathaway
to practise dentistry. One winter he
took all our mother's teeth out in one go,
as she told me three times on a Sunday
quick-marching me to chapel past his house.

And Horeb chapel was a world apart,
containing heaven, the promised land, above,
where Mr Sharp-the-butcher's infant son
dwelt in marble halls with Aunty Martha Jane,
while hell was in the fiery furnace room
that rumbled underneath the vestry floor,
with Sodom and Gomorrah close at hand.
The Halleluiah lamppost marked the end
of the known world in ninety-fifty-eight.

Beyond, the purple-headed mountains,
the terra incognita roamed by boys
on make-shift bikes who brought back travellers' tales,
as fanciful as anthropophagi.

The 9.05 to Paddington, is, as ever, full

You make sure you are sitting comfortably—
window-seat, face forward, phone fully charged,
and you begin a monologue about some knob-head
who only had the nerve to email you,
wants to meet up for a shag. Keeps texting:
calls you Babe and Fudge,
the name they called you in that bar,
the one you used to go to after work,
must have got your number then,
or at that hen do, when you were off your face
and ended up in A&E, but if it's the one you think it is,
the knob-head, he got married last summer
so you've said to him a quick shag is one thing but
what about your wife….

Some words, we note, give your jaw a Mussolini thrust,
and cause an upturn in your voice, which already carries well.

We – your three neighbours – indulge in wishes:
one wishes you could see how hawthorn blossom,
white as summer clothes, moves in a Mexican wave
through the hedgerow running by the track.

Another, who counts every calorie
to keep her weight from getting ideas above its station,
wishes you would ponder each mouthful of baguette
you take when your unseen confessor has her turn.

The third, in the aisle seat beside you,
whose wedding ring was trapped behind arthritis years ago,
wishes you would look and see the wonder of young hands
and marvel at their suppleness.

We, who have learned to love trees and bread and hands,
wish that you, too, could look on beauty
and it would have the power to strike you dumb.

Red Kites

I expected redder than fire engines,
than poisoned apples, lords-and-ladies,
wolves in riding hoods, redder than
a wheelbarrow glazed with rain.

But the gliding shapes seemed dark.

Only as they dropped to Earth
did black change to blood,
blood to rust, rust to sand,
sand to cedar, cedar to auburn,
copper, gold-leaf highlights,
fused in the heat of that astonishing descent.

And that was enough. That was red enough.

Staircases

Who doesn't love
grand buildings
with ammonites
for stairs
curling round
the ram's horn
of the open well
treads
rising in chambers
balusters
like Roman soldiers
shouldering
handrails
of mahogany
deep with elbow grease
landings
falling helter-skelter
to a marble chess-board
of the vestibule
the perfect shape
for standing
arms like wings
head back
spinning on the spot
ears cocked for the
echoes from deep time?

The Great Dustbinian Formation

One day, people will plot,
on the new maps of Earth,
where the fossils are.

They will come
with rock hammers
and collecting bags.

Their palaeontologists
will write learned papers,
four hundred million years from now,
hypothesising how we lived.

Taking the name from
vast deposits we left behind,
they will call us *The Dustbin Age.*

Much will be said about
our signature fossil –
styrofoam pellets – so enduring,
they survived extreme heat
and glaciation intact.

Although too numerous
to be valuable, unlike the leathery
skeletons of extinct life-forms,
nonetheless, stories about them will evolve.

They will be collected
by children who use them in games;
wear them around necks for luck;
tuck them under their pillows for protection.

They will be exchanged
like promises by lovers;
sought by people fearing death
as proof of immortality.

What Love is Like

What a night! Midsummer
and we're half-lost in a wood
of mountain ash and elm
and lovers' leaps to caves
where we can hear
the bats are aestivating.

We totter on a wobble-board
of barely cool volcanoes –
sea-shell fossils crunching underfoot.
The air is so alive, it breathes itself.
And here we are, ankle deep in
orchids and enchanter's nightshade
and I swear that when I looked
I saw you smiling.

Ornithopter

That year, you modelled men with wings,
Stood them on your office window-ledge;

Acquired binoculars to study birds in flight,
Observed the way their feathers hinged and flexed,

How they achieved the proper thrust and lift.
Working late one night, you built a life-sized rig,

Folded and stored it in the cabinet
Assigned for invoices and annual reports.

Your P.A. checked the canvas harness straps,
Tightened buckles, applied the sun-proof gel.

The unfamiliar weight unsettled you
And, for a second, you clung to your desk.

You found walking more natural than standing still,
Although a trifle pigeon-toed at first,

Negotiated door and corridor,
Accelerating somewhere near the stairs.

A passing colleague had the *savoir faire*
To slip the window-catch in time, and waved

As you eased your wings into the sky-blue air,
Spread them to fly upwards and away.

On Going to Lunch with Friends:
One of the Guests Brings Polly, Aged Five Weeks

The women are at the table talking Babies.
A man I knew to be bi-lingual, translates for me:
They are expressing wonder –
  the baby's fingers; the smallness of the toes.

Now they are remembering –
  name bracelets; first shoes; blankets…

The women laugh, a low collective cluck.
A woman I recognise as the one
who brought home-made guacamole
in a covered dish, talks.

My translator whispers:
she is telling a story it is about her mother
embroidering a blanket with ducklings.
The blanket was pink. It was a hint.

But she had two sons.

One of them still lives at home.

The other was buried in his Batman outfit.

He was six.

She is asking if she can hold Polly.

The women gather around her,
closing ranks.

Falling

Tonight's
the slowest
thing that
ever fell.
Falls more slowly
than an egg
dropped in a jar
of isinglass,
a bubble
in a lava lamp,
the priceless
Chinese vase
sent toppling
from a windowsill,
the frail old hip-bone
on the bathroom floor,
my poor heart
through your buttered hands.

Earth

Broad-hipped. Weathered.
Smelling of time before toothpaste and shampoo.
Eyes: loam and coal. Teeth capped with gold.
Earth's a babushka in a paisley shawl.
Hoarder of treasure trove.
Keeper of dirty secrets.
Teller of fairy-tales from ancient forests.
Shelterer of worm and fox.

From seeds and twigs, she feeds all,
Smacks her lips for garlic, parsnip, beetroot –
Food no need to mind your manners for.
Enjoys riddle, rebus and coarse humour.
Receives the dead as if she were a bride
And when she weeps for them, her tears are mud.

The blood of armies, stones of fallen cities
Are ground up in her soil, are the roots of her.
Remembering the hush before mankind,
Fearing for generations yet unborn,
She tramples herself inside our well-kept homes,
Lodges in treads of shoes and boots,
Clings like abandoned children to our hems,
Works her way under finger-nails. Will not be budged.

Fishing

Gary Cooper would have understood,
held our mother in his arms, the day
her bracelet disappeared, and she stood,
sobbing, in the road. Instead,

our father ends up squatting by the outside drain,
poking coat-hangers through the iron grille,
fishing the stinking depths for gold, looking
like a cartoon Eskimo beside a snow-hole.

We mustn't laugh, though. These are the lengths
he's been driven to, sorting out this hoo-ha.
What a move, one deft flick of the wrist and
he's the centre of attention once again.

That tricky heart, the locket that did not hold.
The grief. Gary Cooper would have understood

Nos Galan

When other men were in Masonic halls,
dancing with well-upholstered wives
trussed in Playtex girdles, urged to cross arms,
grab hands, join in Auld Lang Syne, you
were outside, paying out a trail of gunpowder,
running it down the camber of the lane, following
the sound of a stream rising in the hills behind
on its way to the sea which lapped within earshot.
To your left, a dog-fox barked in the woods,
you scanned the sky, looking for signs,
and when you judged it near to midnight,
you struck a match off the sole of your boot
and watched the old year race headlong into the new,
quick enough to catch a bird in flight.

The Nos Galan, or New Year's Eve, race takes place in Mountain
Ash, South Wales. Runners start in one year, and end the in next.

The Fire-Eater's House

Bukhara, 1989

They fill and refill my tea-bowl –
the women who come with butter and meat
and their news from Moscow.

They leave their court-yard houses
with vines and men lolling on day-beds
bring their gifts here
where roads give up
and the desert stretches itself out.

They want to talk about their dreams –
stories from their mothers' mothers' time,
before tanks and cotton-fields and evidence.

Better or worse? they want to know.

I Try Your House on Like Old Clothes

I try your house on like old clothes,
a summer shirt-waist dress in faded shades
of borage and courgette,
four yards of cotton in the skirt,
fabric soft with careful laundering.

In your garden, someone left
a countryman's tweed coat in walnut-brown,
smelling of quince and bonfire,
the pockets full of snow-drop bulbs
and fennel seed – next year's spring.

I leave behind handfuls of well-loved words,
tucked between the piles of pillow-slips,
in double sheets airing by the range, some
roosting on the dresser shelves, the rest suspended
by fine dust in the kitchen air.

Dr Johnson

HE'RO n.s. [heroes, Latin]
    1. A man eminent for bravery
    2. A man of the highest class in any respect

He was a fleshquake of a man who whirred
& clucked & worked his jaw;
who was the butt of school-boy jokes;
coat-front spattered with expectorated snuff;
wig lop-sided, singed by candle flames
held too near to his imperfect eyes.

Melancholic & afraid of idleness,
he stood, for penance, bareheaded in the rain,
for filial disobedience of which he was ashamed.

He shared his narrow house with sundry folk,
& fed Hodge, his cat, with oysters, everyday;
& at his latter end, rejected laudanum
to be unclouded when he settled his account with God.

He was a good & faithful servant to English words,
& kept them fixed & safe between the covers of his book.

St Cuthbert

They acted for the best
Burying him in silk and garnets
And an ivory comb.

By all accounts, he seemed more
The type to dip his hands in water
Plastering down whatever hair
Went haywire round his tonsured head.

More the type to steal away at dusk,
Leave the marble slab, the shrine,
The tracery, the vestments,
The candles, the choir's polyphony
Leave the incense, the panoply,
Give the whole palaver the slip.

And wrap himself in the first
Old cloak that came to hand,
Hunker in a corner of the cloister
Where the pipistrelles, living fur and silk,
Squeeze between the sandstone blocks
And ceiling bosses, ignoring gravity.

Strawberry Thief

At Wightwick Manor

The William Morris pattern
on the parlour chairs
is *Strawberry Thief,*

one of so many treasures
that must be guarded
against so many thieves.

The light-fingered have a field day here,
from those who play the drawing-room piano
(which anyone can see is just for show),

to those who somehow make off
with lead piping, delft-ware colanders,
and tiles. So very portable and moreish.

The daily diminishments by beetles,
mice, mites, dust, and the spider
with its legendary web, make their mark.

It's a siege, a battle, constant warfare.
Even light, left to itself,
would sneak through the casements

and steal away the colour from the rooms,
blue, in particular, has always held it value
on the markets – the open and the black.

Only the clocks are constant here
no force of nature disturbs
the unctuous richness of the clocks

The tick that falls like florins in champagne,
The tock like horn spoons scooping caviare.

Hand Grenades

That autumn, pomegranates were the craze,
Half-each, we harpooned the seeds with pins –

Best friends, in the kitchen, feet on fender,
Taking turns to talk, between neat bites.

What started as cases of baby rubies,
Ended like a drawer of blood-shot eyes;

Our fingers stuck together, our stomachs
Curdled with the awful sweetness.

Now, in tilted boxes outside grocers' shops,
It's time for pomegranates once again.

It feels as if they're urging me to buy,
To catch the scarlet-liveried bus back to the past,

Open the terraced house, search empty rooms,
Rake the ashes in the kitchen grate,

Unlatch the back door, spit out the pin
From the toad-skinned fruit, lob it hard
On the diamond-patterned yard,

Watch it detonate, explode in silver stars,
Defy the season when the clocks fall back.

How to Remember

The trouble with memory
is the interference to cut through
before the picture clears.

Snow, they used to call it
when the screen went fuzzy
on old-fashioned TV sets.

Snow is not one thing, more
a lamination of cross-hatched scraps.
A person with time on their hands

might start steaming the layers
lifting them with tweezers,
naming each one as it comes away,

tracing it to a source: this piece
is from an underground place,
it has the essence of cellar about it;

here's the stuff we used to call *space dust*
still fizzing off the roof of your mouth.
Look, here's a line from a playground game:

Poor Mary sat a-weeping.
Then you reach a puzzle:
what seems to be a scene from a film:

a small girl sits very quietly
in the corner of a cot, watching
as her mother disappears.

You know that's not you. But
how come the girl's hair is tied with a bow
like the ones they made you wear?

Acknowledgements

Borderlines; Mslexia; Obsessed with Pipework; Orbis; Raw Edge; The Cannon's Mouth;The Interpreter's House.

Antholgies: *Wolverhampton Write Now* editors Simon Fletcher and Susan Fearn, Wolverhampton Libaries, 2003; *Bluebeard's Wives,* editors Julie Boden and Zoë Brigley, Heaventree Press, 2007; *Mr Barton Isn't Paying,* editors Meredith Andrea and Jacqui Rowe, Flarestack Poets Pamphlet Anthology, 2009

Also on www.imagetextimage.com;
Radio Wildfire at www.radiowildfire.com

Jane's website: www.janeseabourne.com